Unforced Rhythms of Grace

Rest, Recovery and Flourishing in Ministry

Rhona Knight
Pastoral Supervisor, Spiritual Director,
Retreat Leader and Theological Educator

GROVE BOOKS LIMITED
RIDLEY HALL RD CAMBRIDGE CB3 9HU

Contents

1	Introduction	3
2	Life in its Fullness	6
3	Life and Ministry	8
4	Life Lived Well	13
5	A Life of Love	18
6	Living the Unforced Rhythms of Grace	21
7	Companions on the Journey	24
8	To Conclude	26
	Notes	27

'Are you tired? Worn out? Burned out on religion? Come to me. Get away with me and you'll recover your life. I'll show you how to take a real rest. Walk with me and work with me—watch how I do it. Learn the unforced rhythms of grace. I won't lay anything heavy or ill-fitting on you. Keep company with me and you'll learn to live freely and lightly.'

Matt 11.28-30, The Message

Acknowledgments

Thanks to Drs Jane Marshall, Deborah Cohen, Peter Toon and Michèle Hampson who opened my eyes to ways of promoting well-being and flourishing in life and in the work place. Thanks to Dr Sally Myers who enabled me to develop this teaching and learning in the context of ministry at Lincoln School of Theology. Thanks to St Beuno's in Wales for introducing me to the Ignatian Exercises, which have been a key part of my own unforced rhythms of grace. Thanks to Chris and all the other soul friends I have journeyed with whose stories, experiences and support have been the reason this book has come to be.

First Impression December 2022
ISSN 0144-171X
ISBN 978 1 78827 283 4

1 Introduction

> Blessed be your name in the land that is plentiful
> Blessed be your name when I'm found in the desert place
>
> Matt Redman

Jesus came that we might have abundant life—life in its fullness (John 10.10). Yet many of us, while looking for the gift in adversity and for glimpses of God in times of difficulty, like the psalmist find ourselves overwhelmed with troubles (Ps 88.3). The words of Matt Redman's well-known song above demonstrate these experiences of abundance and of wilderness. Redman echoes the words of Habakkuk encouraging us to rejoice in God even in times of adversity: 'Though the fig tree does not bud and there are no grapes on the vines, though the olive crop fails and the fields produce no food, though there are no sheep in the pen and no cattle in the stalls, yet I will rejoice in the Lord, I will be joyful in God my Saviour' (Hab 3.17–18).

Scripture informs us that while our journey of faith will not be without adversity, God will be with us. As we walk through fire, we will not be burned; as we step through the deep waterways, we will not be overwhelmed (Isa 43.1b–2). Paul highlights the outcome of suffering which produces in turn perseverance, character and hope (Rom 5.3–4). The Holy Week journey of Jesus reminds us that suffering does not have the last word. Psalm 126 reminds us that though we sow in tears we will reap with songs of joy.

Yet while suffering can be seen to have a refining and formative purpose, how can we reconcile this with people's personal, communal and generational experiences of significant trauma—narratives of rape, slavery, torture and other atrocities? How can we hold the promises of God in the times of life when all seems lost and God feels absent? In times of adversity, lasting many, many years, even a lifetime, we may be able to respond like Habakkuk and choose to rejoice. However, we may instead find ourselves, like the author of Psalm 88, only able to cry and lament, being simply aware that, despite everything, there is still someone to lament to. *While Jesus tells us that in his company, even in the worst of places, we can begin to learn his unforced rhythms of grace, and begin to live freely and rightly, for some of us our initial step might be simply to ask to want to learn these unforced rhythms.*

Cracks, Complexity, Context and Ministry

The current climate of Brexit, COVID-19, environmental damage, global warming, sex trafficking, modern-day slavery, war in Ukraine and civil war in Ethiopia has challenged us all and exposed vulnerabilities, globally and locally. Pressured times often bring to light deep work that needs to be done in us as individuals and as community, as cracks become evident in the old patterns and ways that seem to have sustained us. In the context of church, the complex global trauma of COVID-19 has had a significant impact on ways of being church and on ministerial well-being. Tiredness, exhaustion, frustration, anxiety and stress, although affecting all of the priesthood of all believers, were seen more commonly in clergy than laity.[1] Congregations and ministers were often pulled in different directions out of people's desires to return to 'the ways things were' or to rush too quickly into a 'new normal.' How long, O Lord? (Psalm 13). Added to this, shrinking congregations, disillusionment with the establishment, stories of misuse of power, varied new models of ministry and novel initiatives all served to compound the challenge to love God with our heart, soul, mind and strength as individuals and as the body of Christ—and to live the unforced rhythms of grace. *What does flourishing look like in these contexts? Where are the spaces for rest, recovery and hope in times of adversity? What does it mean to walk with and work with God and recover our lives?*

Resilience and Well-being?

For almost two decades now we have heard the word 'resilience' used in church and in secular employment. To cope with the stress and strain in ministry you need to be 'more resilient.' We were taught what to do to make ourselves more resilient. We could build on our natural resilience through negotiating the challenges of life and by regularly using our 'resilience muscles.' Resilience then became weaponized. Employers just needed to provide resilience training and the rest was up to you. If you then developed burnout, it was your fault and not theirs. Resilience became not so much about enabling the wholeness and flourishing of the person and work community, but about avoiding staff taking sick leave. Lack of resilience was portrayed as personal failing, and became a source of stigma and shame, resulting in sidelining and exclusion in ministry. This resonates with the ongoing experiences of those facing physical and mental health challenges in ministry. Canon C4(3) in the Church of England still allows a bishop to exclude a person from holy orders based on the person's past or present 'physical or mental infirmity.'[2]

I have always found resilience in ministry a difficult concept. From my learning at school, resilient objects returned to their normal shape after being stressed and broke beyond the point of return if stressed beyond their elastic limit. This understanding of resilience seemed to leave little space for God's transformation and growth or the impact of community. There are many other factors that impact on how we cope with and survive adversity. Victor Frankl noted that it was attributes like hope, love, beauty and inner freedom rather than bread that enabled survival in Auschwitz. The three stranded cord of Eccl 4.12 conveys the importance of relationships with others and God in adversity. Witnessing how others journey and grow through trauma can also positively change our perspectives and approaches to personal adversity. In the Anglican context, Francis and Village noted that improved spiritual health in COVID-19 was associated with personal, psychological and ecclesial factors. These included being female, older, emotionally stable, of intuitive and feeling types, and being evangelical and charismatic.[3]

Well-being is another concept commonplace in church contexts, but it seems this too is in danger of being hijacked and weaponized in a similar way to resilience. The appointment of a regional or diocesan well-being officer will not necessarily guarantee increased well-being of those in ministry. While evidence does suggest that connecting with others, being physically active, learning new skills, giving to others and paying attention to the present moment improve mental health and well-being, people all start from a different well-being baseline.[4] This baseline can suddenly find itself reset, for example with the news of a family tragedy, unexpected unemployment or illness.

How then can we live as ministers in unforced rhythms of grace? How can we live freely and lightly in companionship with Jesus in all the complexity and mess of modern life? What does it mean to do this in ministry and in companionship with others as we truly love our neighbour as ourselves?

From Surviving to Flourishing

In this Grove booklet we will consider and frame the sacrificial nature of ministry. We will explore a biblical understanding of flourishing and will consider various ways in which flourishing in ministry can become compromised—including burnout, compassion fatigue, vicarious trauma and the negotiation of the multiple boundary issues encountered in everyday church ministry. Informed by Bernard of Clairvaux's four ways of loving God, we will consider good ministerial self-care. Through the words of Psalm 1, we will consider what it means to be planted by water and to continue to live and learn God's unforced rhythms of grace. A link to a downloadable electronic template to an End of Year Examen, which models a structured way for those in all forms of ministry to prayerfully reflect on their personal journey of faith and flourishing, is provided. This template is designed also to be integrated with and inform more formal vocational appraisal processes and ministerial development reviews, if desired. Finally, we will look at two models of confidential reflective space for those in ministry and how to access them.

2 Life in its Fullness

> I am the true vine says the Lord
> As one with me fruitfulness is assured
> With our roots those of Christ,
> Our veins linked with Christ…
>
> Amanda Virgo

Flourishing and Fruitfulness

When you hear the word 'flourishing' what do you imagine? It might be the image of a wisteria covered in flowers, or of a toddler's cheeky face laughing and playing in the water. For others, the image may be of a vine laden with luscious grapes. Vines can have a life of over 50 years, producing harvest after harvest of grapes each summer. While the crop might decrease in later years, old vines are known for producing grapes of a more intense flavour. Following a vine's bud burst, in spring early shoots begin to grow, leading to flowering and fruit setting. This is followed by the grapes changing colour and then ripening, leading to harvest—a flourishing and fruitful vine. How do we hold this image of copious fruitfulness with the realities, struggles and sacrifices of life and ministry where flowers and fruit can seem scarce?

Human flourishing is not the same as happiness, a word sometimes used to capture the concept of blessedness in the Beatitudes and made popular by Martin Seligman and the positive psychology movement (Matt 5.3–12).[5] C S Lewis, in the play *Shadowlands*, links love, pain and suffering, saying, 'God doesn't want us to be happy.'[6] Aristotle explores the concept of *eudaemonia*, the kind of life we should look to live.[7] Peter Toon considers flourishing to be today's best translation of the term *eudaemonia*. Flourishing is, 'a dynamic, botanical metaphor, which incorporates the idea of fulfilment of a purpose but also the shape and narrative of a lifelong purpose.'[8] This meaning has significant overlap with the Hebrew word *shalom* which conveys an idea of completeness, of fulfilment, of things being the way that they should be.

If our definition of flourishing is just limited to lush fruit-laden vines ripe for harvest, we fail to see the whole picture and are in danger of being target- and outcome-driven and failing to understand what it means to be a flourishing vine in the spring, summer, autumn and winter. Picture the vine in winter. It has been pruned. It is devoid of leaves and fruit. No flowers or buds are evident.

Just a barren looking twig for the four months of the year when the vine remains dormant. Yet this dormant twig plays an important dynamic part in *'the shape and narrative of a lifelong purpose.'* Can a dormant vine be said to be flourishing?

As well as different seasons, there are also times of drought. Some vines remain alive through successive years of drought. Are these non-flowering and non-fruiting vines in times of drought flourishing? They are not bearing bad fruit or the wrong fruit (Matt 7.16–20). They are instead waiting for the rain cycle to be restored. If our definition of flourishing is only about fruit production for harvest, we would have to reply no, in times of drought these vines are not flourishing. But what if our definition of flourishing is something more than external appearance and productivity?

It is Well With My Soul

God tells Samuel that unlike people who judge by external appearances, God looks at the heart (1 Sam 16.7). God sees the heart of the dormant vine waiting and resting and being prepared for the next cycle. God sees the heart of the vine in a time of drought holding on for the time of rain that will eventually come. God sees the heart of the fruitful vine as it is being pruned to bear more fruit (John 15.2). The words of the worship song written by Amanda Virgo (above) hint that flourishing is an inner state of being rooted in the vine and in the plans and purposes of God. Flourishing is better seen from an eternal perspective and in the light of the bigger story. I therefore suggest we need to broaden our understanding of flourishing to include *all* the seasons of life—not just the time of harvest. *Flourishing is an inner state of remaining grafted into and so rooted in Christ*. Fruitfulness is assured, but in God's time and in God's way, which we may not appreciate or recognize this side of the grave.

This means that even in winter and in drought, when no fruit is on the vine, if we remain in Christ we are flourishing. We are bare, not barren. We are living a life well lived, in the context in which we have been placed, as we respond to the lifelong call and purposes of God. To take on board this definition of flourishing is countercultural. The question that determines whether you are flourishing is not about how fruitful you, or the ministry you have been called to, are but 'Is it well with your soul?' No matter how fruitful ministry may seem to be, if all is not well with our soul we are not flourishing (John 15.1–8).

Questions to Ponder

- As you look back on your life, what seasons do you notice?
- How has God grown you in the different seasons?
- What is a biblical understanding of flourishing in ministry?
- What season do you feel you are in at the moment?

3 Life and Ministry

> He makes me lie down in green pastures…he restores my soul.
>
> Ps 23.2–3

Patterns of Life

In his classic book of the same name, Dietrich Bonhoeffer wrote of *the cost of discipleship*. Ministry, in the steps of Christ, is sacrificial. Jesus tells us to take up our cross and follow him (Matt 16.24). He also tells us that his yoke is easy and his burden light (Matt 11.28–30). Yet often it does not feel this way. Personal and ministerial life events can feel overwhelming, but when this becomes a pattern for life questions need to be asked. It may be we have accepted unquestioningly the narrative of busyness, failing to take time truly to discern the call of God and instead defaulting to and feeding our various disordered sin patterns. Perfectionism, addiction to work, narcissism, the desire to please, the desire for affirmation or status are just some of the patterns that can result in filling our time and lives with uncalled-for work.

Brokenness, Growth and Mending

Few individuals or families can say that they have not been touched by sorrow. Grief, loss, illness and adversity in their varied forms are part of life. The impact of the past shapes who we are and how we function. It shapes our relationships with others and with God. It shapes the way we understand and live out our faith and how we minister. Throughout life, the challenges of life which we face will also change us. They can help us grow and develop. They can also cause us to develop coping patterns and ways of being that, while initially protective and helpful, can begin to limit us, showing their cracks in later life. Adverse childhood experiences, stressful and potentially traumatic experiences in early life, for example, can have significant effects on relationships, health, opportunity and future experiences of violence.[9] Healing and wholeness are of God, but often what we encounter this side of the grave is the mending of God where the challenges and traumas we have faced leave their scars. We need to be aware of our trigger points, our points of weakness and how in ministry we are wounded healers. It is also wise to have places of accountability and support where we can openly share our vulnerabilities.

Pastoral Ministry

Ezekiel 34 describes the shepherding role of God as one who shepherds with justice; who searches for the sheep and rescues; who gathers the sheep and brings them to his own land; who pastures and tends them; who enables them to lie down in good grazing land, binds the injured and strengthens the weak. This role for God had become necessary because the shepherds of Israel had only taken care of themselves and had ruled harshly and brutally.

We regularly see and hear in the media the experiences of those 'done with church but not with God' because of harsh and brutal shepherds and we personally are likely to know of some people who have experienced pastoral abuse and the actions of wolves in shepherd's clothing. Sometimes the behaviours are intentional but in many toxic shepherds there is a lack of awareness not only of how much they are deeply-loved, forgiven sinners but also of their own narcissism, brokenness and fear.

While some do seek to enter Christian ministry for perverse motives, most are wanting to seek, hear and follow God's call, despite their frailty and lack of clarity of their true motives. While, for some, ministry has been a way to an easy life, working 'one day a week' and living in luxurious, paid-for housing, for others, like shepherds out in the fields during lambing season, church ministry can see sleep sacrificed, holidays precluded and more time spent away from family than desired. Tied housing may be poor or in an area where it is unsafe to walk out at night, with the wider implications of this on personal and family life.

As well as risking life to protect sheep from predators, many in ministry can tell stories of having been subjected to a 'sheep attack' or of suffering from misuse of power and bullying from others in ministry and from those within ecclesiastical structures.[10] For those who, like Paul, are 'tent-making,' where a paid job is used to support working within the church context, time for family and for leisure is compromised. For those 'living by faith' there is often the continued existence in a place of uncertainty as to where the next meal or children's school uniform is coming from. For some shepherds, the demands of the job can mean that it is all too easy for perspectives to become distorted and the work and role of shepherd to take the place of God as objects of worship. Overwork, failure to spend time with God and a culture of busyness can prevail. The tendency of some churches to put those in leadership on a pedestal can fuel narcissistic tendencies and facilitate abuse and misuse of power.

Compassion Fatigue

As with other vocations, the characteristics that can make a person naturally good at pastoral work can, with the nature, volume and context of ministry, predispose them to *compassion fatigue*. Working with people who have been traumatized places professionals at risk of burnout, compassion fatigue and vicarious trauma.[11] *Compassion fatigue* is diagnosed as being due to a combination of *burnout* and *vicarious traumatic stress*.[12] Emotional exhaustion is well recognized in teaching[13] and ways of improving mental health and well-being for teachers are seen to be important.[14] Compassion fatigue is well recognized in health care[15] and social work and proactive approaches to self-care and healthy work environments are encouraged.[16] While there is little research in the UK on compassion fatigue, burnout and vicarious trauma in church ministry, St Luke's Hospital for the Clergy[17] and the Society of Mary and Martha at Sheldon demonstrate how the wider church is now increasingly concerning itself with supporting ministers.[18]

Burnout

A helpful definition of *burnout* is: 'a depletion or exhaustion of a person's mental and physical resources attributed to his or her prolonged yet unsuccessful striving toward unrealistic expectations, internally or externally derived.'[19] Burnout can be the result of difficult work environments and things outside an individual's control. The Copenhagen Burnout Inventory is a validated and reliable free tool to assess levels of burnout.[20] Factors known to increase the likelihood of burnout resonate with many in church ministry: high workload; high stress contexts; being on the front line; lack of autonomy; powerlessness; lack of resources; feelings of being stuck with lack of opportunities for growth, development and promotion; perceived injustice; value conflicts and feelings of isolation and disconnection from family and friends due to the nature of the work being done.[21] Strategies to enable awareness of and to address developing burnout are available but can be difficult, especially for ministers who live on the job. These strategies include a balance between professional (vocational) and personal needs, creative outlets, good end-of-work rituals, good sleep, nutrition and exercise regimes, avoiding gambling and self-medicating with alcohol, having good support systems and appropriately accessing medical or psychological help.[22]

Vicarious Trauma

Vicarious trauma is seen in a variety of professional roles and is the result of the empathic engagement with another person's traumatic narrative. The professional may develop symptoms of traumatic responses, post-traumatic responses, anxiety, depression and other mental health challenges.[23] These reactions are seen to be more severe when the triggers of trauma have been perpetrated by people rather than by natural disasters.[24] McCann and Pearlman note that those working with people experiencing trauma can themselves experience a shattering of assumptions about self and the world which can result in long-lasting schema changes.[25] Those in church ministry often work with people who have experienced trauma, for example through food banks, homeless and debt action charities, and rehousing of refugees. They are therefore at risk of vicarious trauma. The impact of vicarious trauma is multi-faceted and includes anxiety, agitation, depression, sadness, anger and impact on working relationships.[26] Pearlman identifies three ways of preventing vicarious trauma—awareness, balance and connection.[27] Babette Rothschild's *Help for the Helper* seeks to enable effective self-care of people empathically engaging in caring and helping roles.[28]

Moral Injury

In cases where the church has been the cause of traumatic experiences, for example through clergy or church officers perpetrating or failing to deal appropriately with abuse, there is the significant and wider impact of a shattering of assumptions[29] relating to the expectation that the church will reflect their understanding of a good / compassionate / loving / just God and through disbelief that the church could behave in a particular ungodly way.[30] This may be accompanied by a shattering of assumptions relating to concepts of God. The term 'moral injury' is used to describe these strong emotional and cognitive responses which occur when events happen that do violence to a person's deeply held values, beliefs and desired ways of living—their moral code. This can happen when people, or the organization to which they belong, fail to act in a way which resonates with their own values. An example could be seeing a ministerial colleague being discriminated against and victimized by an archdeacon or bishop but choosing to stay silent to protect their own career. Betrayal by trusted others can also result in moral injury.

Moral injury can result in significantly compromised well-being, distress, guilt, shame, altered belief systems, withdrawal, self-harm and poor coping strategies such as substance misuse.[31] It is associated with post-traumatic stress disorder, depression and suicide.[32]

Vicarious Resilience

Working and walking with people journeying through adversity can have a positive effect. McCann and Pearlman identified various positive effects of trauma work including a more realistic view of the world and increased sense of meaning, empathy, compassion, knowledge of contexts of violence, motivation towards social action, improved self-esteem, and a sense of hope coming from seeing people endure and overcome traumatic experiences.[33] 'Vicarious resilience' is the term currently used to describe this.[34] Edith Eger's book *The Choice* is a classic text demonstrating growth through trauma. Eger, a holocaust survivor who became a psychotherapist working with Vietnam war veterans, conveys a strong sense of hope, meaning and post-traumatic growth in her writing.[35]

Vicarious Trust

I propose another vicarious impact of journeying with others through life in its adversity: vicarious trust. Ministers are privileged to bear witness to the many stories of God at work in the lives of others in times of plenty and in the hard places. We bear witness to people's deep recognition of the actions and presence of God—this loving, all-powerful God who is absolutely trustworthy. Just as the Israelites' remembrance of the acts of God in the past could help them trust God for the future, our seeing the work of the Holy Spirit and the presence of God in the lives of others can inspire and change us for the future, helping us to avoid trying to retain control but instead to trust in God.

Questions to Ponder

- What is my vision of pastoral care and ministry?
- What patterns of life do I have that compromise my well-being?
- How does my current context compromise or enhance my well-being?
- How have I been affected by compassion fatigue and vicarious trauma?
- How have I been affected by vicarious resilience and vicarious trust?
- Where do I discern areas of moral injury in my own life?

4

Life Lived Well

> When peace like a river attendeth my way
> When sorrows like sea billows roll
> Whatever my lot, Thou hast taught me to say
> It is well, it is well with my soul
>
> Horatio Spafford

Living Faithfully

What does a well-lived life look like?

Examples we might turn to are the Polish priest Maximilian Kolbe who volunteered to die in place of another man in Auschwitz; Mother Teresa who founded the Missionaries of Charity, and who was no stranger to spiritual dryness; John of the Cross, the Spanish Carmelite friar and mystic poet who, as a supporter of reform was taken prisoner, kept in a stifling cell under a brutal regime, and publicly whipped until his escape.

Further examples of lives lived well might include those who minister in more hidden ways, such as the fictional character Dorothea in *Middlemarch*. George Eliot concludes 'But the effect of her being on those around her was incalculably diffusive: for the growing good of the world is partly dependent on unhistoric acts; and that things are not so ill with you and me as they might have been, is half owing to the number who lived faithfully a hidden life, and rest in unvisited tombs.'[36]

Our Chief End

For many of us there is the temptation to want to do great things for God—to become another Mother Theresa or Billy Graham. This can become what drives us, when Jesus calls us simply to walk and work with him and let him grow the fruit. The Westminster Shorter Catechism begins by stating that our chief end is to glorify God, and to enjoy him forever. The Ignatian First Principle and Foundation says that God created human beings to praise, reverence and serve God. God is the focus of a life well-lived. Jesus summarizes it as '*seek first the kingdom of God*' (Matt 6.33). In this chapter, I suggest that seeking to love the Lord our God with all our heart, soul, mind and strength enables us to keep glorifying God as our focus, helps us to remain secure in the vine and ensures we flourish. This in turn results in a heart inclined to love God and neighbour and truly to love self—an embodied life of love, lived out in community.

Spiritual disciplines, rules of life and Sabbath are all ways that can help us love God. The Benedictine way, for example, emphasizes the need for prayer, work, study and leisure. Quiet time and retreat encourage us to carve out quality time with God. Noticing God at work in the everyday encourages thankfulness. Jesus asks us to walk with him and work with him, dwelling on what is noble, right and true (Phil 4.8). However, ministerial life is full of boundary areas that can find us walking away from God's perfect will before we realize it.

Boundaries and Ministry

Physical boundaries come in many shapes and sizes. They can mark a territory. They can protect things within and keep other things out. They can be clear or unclear.

When we minister, we encounter boundaries. Jesus kept and transgressed boundaries. He regularly withdrew to a quiet place to be with his Father. He indicated to his mother at Cana that his time was not yet come. He challenged the Gentile woman seeking healing for her daughter about giving the food meant for Israel to those who are not of Israel. Respecting boundaries that are wise and godly prevents us wandering, enabling us to stay rooted in the vine, walking and working with God. Maintaining inappropriate boundaries can result in us finding excuses to avoid the call of God. Problems arise in ministry when boundaries are ignored, used to hide or protect the *status quo*, not recognized or not duly considered. While boundaries can be and sometimes need to be crossed, to do so must be done intentionally, prayerfully, wisely and appropriately.

Boundaries and the Bible

Biblical boundaries take many forms. There are 'if…then…' laws (2 Chron 7.14). There are divine laws, the Ten Commandments and the greatest commandment(s) being examples. The Bible also gives us boundary guidance through the *principles* that it espouses, as in Rom 14.13–19. *Paradigms* that we can infer from the whole story of Scripture increase our understanding of God and of humanity. *Moral example stories* teach us that individual stories should not be interpreted as normative behaviour, but instead understood in the wider context of the story of God. The wider biblical context of the narratives of Bathsheba and of the dismembered concubine is of all women being equal in the eyes of God to free men and not objects to be raped and abused.

Boundaries and the Church

Boundaries in church ministry are important and are usually seen to enable and promote safety. The consistency, clarity, accountability, openness, transparency, care and honesty mentioned by Justin Welby are good indicators of the kinds of boundaries needed for ministers and the church as a whole.[37] Boundaries, however, can also be harmful when they become barriers to the good. Such barriers can be intentionally or unintentionally created and can be used to hide misdemeanours and even to enable and perpetrate abuse. As IICSA highlighted, 'The culture of the Church of England facilitated it becoming a place where abusers could hide. Deference to the authority of the Church and to individual priests, taboos surrounding discussion of sexuality and an environment where alleged perpetrators were treated more supportively than victims presented barriers to disclosure that many victims could not overcome.'[38]

Expectations and Boundaries

What are your expectations of ministry and what are the expectations of those you minister with and to? Differing expectations are common causes of conflict and often relate to boundaries. In their 'Safer Sacred Spaces' training programme[39] the United Reformed Church asks its ministers to consider realistic and unrealistic expectations through a ministerial expectations questionnaire.[40]

Everyday Boundaries

Boundary areas are places of increased risk. They are places where it is easy to misuse power. They are also places of creativity and growth. For most ministers it is usually not the big boundary issues that lead to problems but failing to discern and negotiate the smaller boundaries of everyday ministry in the church. Many forms of church ministry are described as being 'on the edge.' You can download a PDF with 30 common, but often unrecognized, boundary scenarios from the Grove website or at the QR code to the right. In each case try to identify what types of boundary issue are raised. Example areas might include time, money, space, dual roles, conflicts of interest, self-care, self-disclosure, confidentiality, touch, sexual involvement and place. Then consider how you might approach each issue *in your own context*. You might find it helpful to discuss some of these in your ministry team or with colleagues, noting how different people and contexts can impact on how each situation is approached.

Identifying and Safely Negotiating the Boundary Areas

I want to suggest three key elements to safely negotiating boundaries: awareness, reflective space and discernment.

Awareness

Many people come to ministry with a keen awareness of boundary issues and the use and misuse of power from previous careers such as education, social work and counselling. Others coming to ministry are more boundary naive. Whatever the background we come from, ministry will pose new boundary issues in various shapes and sizes. Developing the skills to notice them requires us to have taken time to consider what they might be. The scenarios at the QR link above aim to raise awareness as you consider a few of the many issues you might encounter in ministry. Awareness requires us to notice our responses—emotional, cognitive, spiritual and physical. Bodily responses can be key ways of discerning that we are entering boundary territory. As a pastoral supervisor, I find my body knows we have entered boundary territory before my brain and emotions catch up. I feel tension in my neck, butterflies in my stomach and my heart rate increases. I feel as if there is a fork in what has thus far been a clear road, and I am in a place of choice.

Reflective Space

Reflective spaces in ministry are important—to celebrate, to explore experience and to consider more concerning areas in ministerial practice, including boundary issues. These reflective spaces are places where we can be vulnerable, open and supported. They usually take place in a confidential safe space, in protected time, with clear contracting and regular review. Reflective practice groups, Balint-style groups, peer support groups and pastoral supervision all provide such spaces.[41] These allow reflection on actions and experiences in the light of the journey of faith and ministry. They enable reception of insights from others and consideration of how to move forward. In his book *The Reflective Practitioner*, Donald Schon also talks about the importance of reflection before and during action.[42] For many this becomes a dialogue with God as we prepare, as we act and as we look back.

Discernment

Once a boundary issue has been identified, the challenge is to discern what to do. This may be obvious—for example a clear church gifts policy. However, discernment is often more complex and cannot be covered by a list of rules. In these situations, knowing what the boundaries are, for example ministerial codes of practice, safeguarding guidance and the law of the land can help us navigate through. Knowing with whom we should discuss different areas of uncertainty is essential, be that a safeguarding advisor, a line manager or a pastoral supervisor. Discernment is also a gift of the Spirit. Cultivating a discerning spirit is part of the journey of faith, and many ministers of all traditions have found the Examen explicitly brings God in to our refléction at the end of each day and helps us learn to discern how we walk with and walk away from God in the warp and weft of daily life.[43] In boundaries that are about ethical issues the following seven-step process can help discern what to do and how to move forward both individually and as part of a group process.

1 Commit the decision-making process to God, asking the Holy Spirit to help you discern his will and direction.
2 Identify clearly what the boundary issue is.
3 Identify what knowledge you need before a decision can be made, and consider who else you might talk with.
4 Consider what personal and professional values, laws and regulations need to inform decision making.
5 Consider how Scripture and your experience of God can shed light on the decision.
6 Decide how to move forward in a clear and justifiable way.
7 Bring this decision before God.

Questions to Ponder

- What boundary issues do I encounter regularly?
- How do I deal with them?
- What boundary issues do I find most challenging?
- What boundary issues can I be blind to?
- What confidential reflective spaces do I have to consider boundary issues?

5

A Life of Love

Jesus replied: '"Love the Lord your God with all your heart and with all your soul and with all your mind." This is the first and greatest commandment. And the second is like it: "Love your neighbour as yourself." All the Law and the Prophets hang on these two commandments.'

Matt 22.37–40

On Loving God

There are many ways of conceiving how we love God, others and self. Bernard of Clairvaux in *On Loving God* writes, 'And because love is natural, it is only right to love the Author of nature first of all.'[44] Bernard then goes on to note how the frailty of human nature means that instead we turn to love ourselves first. On loving our neighbour, he notes, 'Now a man cannot love his neighbour in God, except he love God himself; wherefore we must love God first, in order to love our neighbours in him.'

Bernard then writes of four 'degrees' of love:[45]

- The first degree of love—selfish love—where we love God for our self's sake. 'In such wise man, animal and carnal by nature, and loving only himself, begins to love God by reason of that very self-love; since he learns that in God he can accomplish all things that are good, and that without God he can do nothing.'
- The second degree of love—depending on God—where we love God for our own blessing. 'No longer do we love God because of our necessity, but because we have tasted and seen how gracious the Lord is.'
- The third degree of love—intimacy with God—where we love God for God's own sake. 'Whosoever praises God for his essential goodness, and not merely because of the benefits he has bestowed, does really love God for God's sake, and not selfishly.'
- The fourth degree of love—loving self to love God—where we love ourselves for God's sake. 'How blessed is he who reaches the fourth degree of love, wherein one loves himself only in God!'

For Bernard, our reason for loving God is 'God himself; and the measure of love due to him is immeasurable love.' We will be possessed by the fourth degree of love, he says, when our soul has been clothed with our new body which is spiritual, immortal, perfect, lovely and, in everything, fully subject to the Spirit. This is not attainable through our effort but is a gift of God. Bernard's fourth degree of love provides a way of approaching and framing self-care in a congruent, integrative and God-focused way.

Loving Self for God's Sake

Self-care is topical. It is seen as a key to promoting well-being. It is often spoken of in the context of work-life balance. The problem is that self-care can become yet another list of things to do. In seeking to balance the *scales of life* we can place so much work on one side of the balance scales and so much life on the other that the scales break. It is also all too easy for the focus of self-care or work-life balance to become an idol. Bernard's fourth degree of love, loving ourselves for God's own sake, beautifully reframes this.

What I am suggesting here is a different way of approaching the modern concept of self-care and well-being, using the greatest commandment as a guide. In this, our focus is on loving ourselves as a part of loving God. Love of God becomes our aim and not our own well-being. No longer is sabbath time seen as time off, but instead as an act of worship. No longer is going to the gym seen as something to do to stay healthy, but is seen as an act of caring for the temple of the Holy Spirit. *Acts of self-love are first about loving God.*

Using Dallas Willard's description of the soul as 'the part of our being that integrates and enlivens everything going on in the various dimensions of the self,' self-care becomes soul-care as we seek to remain grafted into and so rooted in Christ.[46] As we seek to love God with all that we are, heart, soul, mind and body, we increasingly embody, individually and in the body of Christ, what it truly means to love ourselves. There may be times when we are called to costly living. What it means to love God with our bodies when we have a chronic degenerative illness will be different from when we are at the prime of physical fitness. What it means to love God with our minds when we are studying for exams will be different from when we are well established in a career. What remains the same is the call to love God with our whole being in community.

Questions to Ponder

- How well do I steward the heart, soul, mind and body God has given me?
- What does it mean to be to be part of the body of Christ?

- How do I care for the people and relationships in my life?
- How do I love myself for the sake of loving God?
- How might I love myself more for the sake of loving God?
- What changes do I think God might be inviting me to step in to?

6 Living the Unforced Rhythms of Grace

> Blessed is the one...whose delight is in the law of the Lord, and who meditates on his law day and night. That person is like a tree planted by streams of water, which yields its fruit in season...
>
> Psalm 1

Living Water

When you picture the tree in Psalm 1, what do you imagine? I am taken to a beautiful old willow tree in the town where I grew up, standing proudly where the river splits in two to border the meadowland. However, the Judean hill country and wilderness are different from the green pastureland of the UK, as are the tree populations and water supply. Due to the nature, geology and shape of the Holy Land, some parts are blessed with abundant water and others are not. Living water is cool spring water that arises when water that has fallen on the hills bubbles out from cracks in the rock. Well water comes from the water table, fed each year by the early and late rains. The land and its water supply dictate what flourishes where. Issues of lack of water are addressed intentionally. In the time of Jesus, this included the use of cisterns to collect water during the rainy season; land irrigation to enable crops to grow; and aqueducts to direct the flow of water to where it was needed.

Teresa of Avila wrote of four different ways of watering the garden of our prayer relationship with God. Three of these require effort on our part. The fourth is pure gift of God. Her first way is with well water. Drawing water this way is 'very laborious.' The second way is where water is 'raised by means of an engine and buckets, drawn by a windlass.' This is 'a less troublesome way than the first.' Teresa's third, 'much better' way is by a stream or brook. Here 'the soil is more thoroughly saturated, and there is no necessity to water it so often, and the labour of the gardener is much less.' The final way is 'by showers of rain, when our Lord himself waters it, without labour on our part—and this way is incomparably better than all the others of which I have spoken.' We can do nothing to make this happen—we just wait and receive.[47]

In John 4, Jesus offers the woman by the well living water. Water gushes forth from the temple in Ezekiel 47. Revelation 22 describes the river of life. The tree of Psalm 1 is planted by water. Living water brings life. What we do not know about the tree in Psalm 1 is if the stream is a natural stream or a created irrigation channel. What the water supply in the Holy Land and Teresa's four waters of prayer do tell us is that sometimes we need to be intentional in creating ways in our lives to receive the living water of Jesus. Cisterns, wells and irrigation channels have their role to hold and channel water. While rain can happen at any time and the Spirit blows where she wills, retreats can function as cisterns, gathered worship as a well and a rule of life as an irrigation channel, for example.

Cisterns, Wells and Irrigation Channels

It is helpful to take time regularly to reflect how well-watered the different aspects of our lives are and consider prayerfully where changes might be needed. Two possible approaches can be found below. The first is the water wheel and the second is an end of year Examen. Both can be done informally or included partially or fully as part of an annual appraisal or ministerial review process if desired.

The Water Wheel

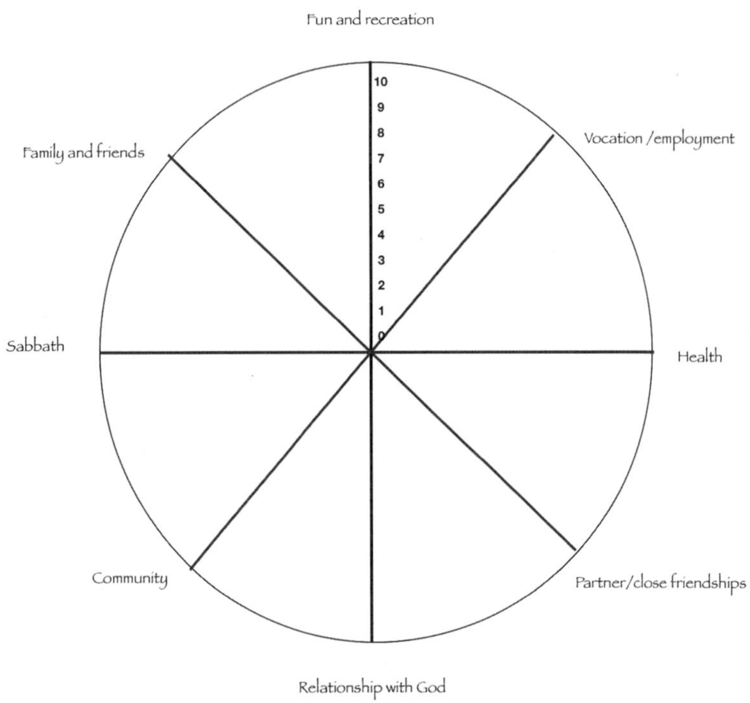

Take a look at the waterwheel opposite or at the QR code link. As you do so, ask the Holy Spirit to guide, lead and bring insight.

- On a scale of 0–10, where 0 is poorly watered and 10 is well-watered, how well-watered are the different dimensions of your life?
- Plot these on the wheel.
- Draw the dots together and consider what you see.
- In what areas of life are you thirsty for living water?
- What kinds of wells, cisterns and irrigation channels might you need to make to ensure adequate water supply?
- How might God be inviting you to do this?
- How do you respond?

End of Year Examen

The QR code to the right below takes you to a template of an End of Year Examen. The suggestion is that you use this once a year to reflect prayerfully on how you are loving yourself for the sake of loving God. Good times to do this can be during Advent or Lent or at the beginning of the academic or calendar year.

Questions to Ponder

- What do I think and feel about this chapter?
- What are my wells, cisterns and irrigation channels?
- How might I incorporate the water wheel into my life and ministry?
- What are my reactions to allocating protected time to do an end of year Examen each year?
- When would be the best time in the year for me to do this?
- What might get in the way and how could this be overcome?

7 Companions on the Journey

It is Not Good for People to be Alone

Supportive relationships where we can be encouraged and challenged are important in ministry. Peer supervision, peer reflection and Balint-style groups are all examples of these. In this chapter, I want to highlight two different professional companions who might accompany you on your ministerial journey—a pastoral supervisor and a spiritual director. These roles cover different areas of life and many people have both. While a counsellor, a mentor, a psychotherapist or a coach may also be beneficial companions at times on the ministerial journey, these relationships are often shorter term and for a season. In times of crisis, GPs and other sources of emergency support are also often needed.[48]

A Pastoral Supervisor

Pastoral supervision offers a protected and confidential space that gives you time to reflect on your ministry with a trained pastoral supervisor and to come to your own conclusions before God. Implicit in this is the acknowledgment of a desire to mature and grow in your journey of faith and ministerial practice. It is a regular, planned and intentional meeting that takes place in protected time to enable you to look at your practice. While theological reflection is the cornerstone of the process, pastoral supervision also focuses on personal awareness, psychological reflection, practitioner skills and professional development. It is characterized by a relationship of support, openness, trust, confidentiality and challenge, where you are given freedom and space to explore issues arising from your different roles. It is a process that encourages and enables personal growth and development. Pastoral supervision is sensitive to context, and is rooted in practice. It attends to the variety of areas that impact on work and role including fitness to practice, skills, boundaries and professional identity.

A Spiritual Director

Spiritual direction (or spiritual accompaniment) is often seen as a covenant relationship. It is the listening and enabling presence, set within the context of a mutual relationship, given by one Christian to another which enables the person being accompanied to notice, discover and pay attention to God's presence and leading in their day-to-day lives. It enables and encourages the person being accompanied to reflect on, respond to and grow in intimacy with God. The person being accompanied is supported to grow in inner freedom in God and in the development of their prayer life. Spiritual direction is a way of creating space to help us to see and hear the real director, the Holy Spirit.

Finding the Right Person

Deciding who to accompany you is important. Some people choose these companions from outside of the area in which they are working to avoid or minimize dual roles, confidentiality issues and conflicts of interest. Others have supervision and direction mandated as part of their ministerial role. You should expect pastoral supervisors and spiritual directors to be properly trained, insured and supervised. There should be a clear contract and regular review. The London Centre for Spiritual Direction[49] and The Association of Pastoral Supervision and Education websites provide further information.[50]

Questions to Ponder

- Who are my closest companions on the journey of faith?
- What confidential spaces do I have to reflect on my life with God?
- What confidential spaces do I have to reflect on ministry?
- Are these spaces working well?
- What changes might I need to make?

8

To Conclude

Recovering Your Life

> But the fruit of the Spirit is love, joy, peace, forbearance, kindness, goodness, faithfulness, gentleness and self-control. Against such things there is no law.
>
> Gal 5.22–23

Maranatha

In this booklet we have looked at life and ministry, identifying how factors such as who we are, the nature of our ministry and our wider context can result in negative impacts like burnout and vicarious trauma and positive impacts like vicarious resilience and trust. I have suggested we need to define flourishing in ministry as *an inner state of remaining grafted into and so rooted in Christ*, whatever the season. We have explored how awareness, reflection and discernment can enable us to retain healthy ministerial boundaries. We have reframed self-care as being about loving ourselves for the sake of loving God and have been encouraged to look at how we can apply this in our own lives. We have looked at the watering of the tree in Psalm 1 and considered how we might intentionally create ways and spaces for us to receive the living water of God. We have considered companions we might choose to accompany us on the journey to enable us to reflect and consider our relationship with God and our ministerial practice.

In *The Message* translation of Matt 11.28, given at the start of this booklet, Jesus asks three questions: Are you tired? Worn out? Burned out on religion?

- What are your answers?

Jesus then invites us to come, get away, walk with, work with, watch, learn and keep company with him.

- Which part of his invitation do you feel drawn to respond to?
- What will that response be?
- What grace do you want to ask from God to help you on that journey?

Notes

1 https://www.yorksj.ac.uk/media/content-assets/document-directory/documents/CoE-Covid-19--Church-21-Churches-and-Clergy-report.pdf (accessed 21 August 2022).
2 https://www.churchofengland.org/about/leadership-and-governance/legal-services/canons-church-england/section-c (accessed 21 August 2022).
3 https://www.churchtimes.co.uk/articles/2022/22-july/comment/opinion/benefits-of-soul-care-are-more-than-spiritual (accessed 21 August 2022).
4 https://www.nhs.uk/mental-health/self-help/guides-tools-and-activities/five-steps-to-mental-well-being/ (accessed 21 August 2022).
5 M Seligman, *Flourish: A New Understanding of Happiness and Well-being—and How to Achieve Them* (London: Nicholas Brealey, 2011).
6 W Nicholson, *Shadowlands* (1989).
7 J A K Thomson (trans), Aristotle, *The Ethics of Aristotle: The Nicomachean Ethics* (Harmondsworth: Penguin, 1955).
8 P D Toon, *A Flourishing Practice?* (London: Royal College of General Practitioners, 2014).
9 http://www.healthscotland.scot/population-groups/children/adverse-childhood-experiences-aces/overview-of-aces (accessed 21 August 2022).
10 D R Maynard, *When Sheep Attack* (USA: BookSurge Publishers, 2010).
11 For example I L McCann and L A Pearlman, 'Vicarious traumatization: a framework for understanding the psychological effects of working with victims,' *Journal of Traumatic Stress* 1990; 3(1): 131–149.
12 B H Stamm, C R Figley, 'Advances in the theory of compassion satisfaction and fatigue and its measurement with the ProQOL 5,' International Society for Traumatic Stress Studies 2009 annual conference, Atlanta, GA in S Megan Berthold, *Vicarious Trauma and Resilience* (Kindle Book, NetCE, 2020) p 53. See also http://compassionfatigue.org/pages/ProQOLManualOct05.pdf (accessed 21 August 2022).
13 A Philipp and H Schüpbach, 'Longitudinal effects of emotional labour on emotional exhaustion and dedication of teachers,' *Journal Occupational Health Psychology* 2010; 15(4): 494–504.
14 https://igpp.org.uk/event/improving-mental-health-and-well-being-for-teachers-and-teaching-staff (accessed 21 August 2022).
15 R Knight, 'The doctor, the patient and compassion,' *Journal of Holistic Healthcare* 2011; 8(3): 50–53.
16 https://www.som.org.uk/social-workers-risk-compassion-fatigue (accessed 21 August 2022).
17 https://www.stlukesforclergy.org.uk (accessed 21 August 2022).
18 https://www.sheldonretreat.com (accessed 21 August 2022).
19 H J Freudenberger, 'Impaired clinicians: coping with burnout' in P A Keller and L Ritt (eds), *Innovations in Clinical Practice: A Source Book*, Vol 3 (Sarasota, FL: Professional Resource Exchange, 1984) pp 223–227.
20 https://nfa.dk/da/Vaerktoejer/Sporgeskemaer/Sporgeskema-til-maaling-af-udbraendthed/Copenhagen-Burnout-Inventory-CBI (accessed 21 August 2022).
21 B H Stamm (ed), *Secondary Traumatic Stress: Self-Care Issues for Clinicians, Researchers, and Educators*, 2nd edn (Lutherville, MD: Sidran Press, 1999).
22 Freudenberger, *op cit.*
23 J P Wilson and J D Lindy (eds), *Countertransference in the Treatment of PTSD* (New York: Guilford Press, 1994).
24 *ibid.*

25 I L McCann and L A Pearlman, *Psychological Trauma and the Adult Survivor: Theory, Therapy, and Transformation* (New York: Brunner/Mazel, 1990).
26 *ibid.*
27 https://youtu.be/wVDSdta0mbM (accessed 21 August 2022).
28 B Rothschild, *Help for the Helper: The Psychophysiology of Compassion Fatigue and Vicarious Trauma* (New York: W W Norton, 2006).
29 R Janoff-Bulman, *Shattered Assumptions: Towards a New Psychology of Trauma* (New York: Free Press, 1992) referenced in S Megan Berthold, *Vicarious Trauma and Resilience, op cit,* p 53.
30 Janet Fife and Gilo (eds), *Letters to a Broken Church* (London: Ekklesia, 2019) and https://www.iicsa.org.uk/document/anglican-church-safeguarding-church-england-and-church-wales-investigation-report (accessed 21 August 2022).
31 https://www.thelancet.com/action/showPdf?pii=S2215-0366%2821%2900113-9 (accessed 21 August 2022).
32 V Williamson, S A M Stevelink and N Greenberg, 'Occupational moral injury and mental health: systematic review and meta-analysis,' *British Journal of Psychiatry* 2018; 212(6): 339–346.
33 I L McCann and L A Pearlman, 'Vicarious traumatization: a framework for understanding the psychological effects of working with victims,' *Journal of Traumatic Stress* 1990; 3(1): 131–149.
34 https://www.researchgate.net/profile/Pilar-Hernandez-Wolfe/publication/274237621_Vicarious_Resilience_Vicarious_Trauma_and_Awareness_of_Equity_in_Trauma_Work/links/5559333508ae980ca610661a/Vicarious-Resilience-Vicarious-Trauma-and-Awareness-of-Equity-in-Trauma-Work.pdf (accessed 21 August 2022) and K W Saakvitne, H Tennen and G Affleck, 'Exploring thriving in the context of clinical trauma theory: constructivist self development theory,' *Journal of Social Issues* 1998; 54(2): 279–299.
35 E Eger, *The Choice* (London: Rider, 2018).
36 G Eliot, *Middlemarch* (Ware: Wordsworth, 1993).
37 J Welby, 'Personal statement from Archbishop Justin Welby on Bishop George Bell,' 17 November 2021: https://www.archbishopofcanterbury.org/news/news-and-statements/personal-statement-archbishop-justin-welby-bishop-george-bell (accessed 21 August 2022).
38 https://www.iicsa.org.uk/reports-recommendations/publications/investigation/anglican-church/executive-summary (accessed 21 August 2022).
39 https://urc.org.uk/images/D_Education_Learning.pdf (accessed 21 August 2022).
40 https://bit.ly/3CnLgVE (accessed 21 August 2022).
41 https://www.tandfonline.com/doi/abs/10.1558/prth.v1i1.95 (accessed 21 August 2022).
42 D Schon, *The Reflective Practitioner* (New York: Basic Books, 1983).
43 https://www.vineyardchurches.org.uk/wp-content/uploads/2020/05/The-Daily-Examen-Card_Revised.jpg (accessed 21 August 2022).
44 Bernard of Clairvaux, *On Loving God*, available at https://www.ccel.org/ccel/b/bernard/loving_god/cache/loving_god.pdf (accessed 21 August 2022).
45 *ibid,* written in the twefth century.
46 D Willard, *Renovation of the Heart: Putting on the Character of Christ* (London: IVP, 2002) p 199.
47 St Teresa of Avila, *Life of St Teresa of Jesus, of The Order of Our Lady of Carmel*, Chapter XI:11ff available at https://ccel.org/ccel/teresa/life/life (accessed 22 August 2022).
48 Places to access help and support may be found at https://bit.ly/3CkgEnL
49 https://www.lcsd.org.uk (accessed 21 August 2022).
50 https://www.pastoralsupervision.org.uk (accessed 21 August 2022).